D0983269

DISCARDED
FROM
LIU LIBRARY

INSTRUCTIONAL

IMc
MEDIA
CENTER

C.W. POST CAMPUS OF L.I.U.

SAVE MY RAINFOREST

Monica Zak

Illustrations by Bengt-Arne Runnerström

English version by Nancy Schimmel

VOLCANO
· PRESS ·

Volcano, California

English language edition published 1992 by Volcano Press, Inc.
English language text © 1992 by Volcano Press, Inc., USA.
All rights reserved.

First published in the Swedish language in 1989 with the title **RÄDDA MIN DJUNGEL**
by Bokförlaget Opal
© Text: Monica Zak 1987
Illustrations by Bengt-Arne Runnerström 1987
Printed in Denmark

SAVE MY RAINFOREST is available in a Spanish language edition under the title
SALVEN MI SELVA from:

Iaconi Book Imports
1110 Mariposa Street
San Francisco, CA 94107

Library of Congress Cataloging-in-Publication Data

Zak, Monica, 1939-
    [Rädda min djungel. English]
    Save my rainforest / by Monica Zak ; illustrated by Bengt-Arne Runnerström ; English
version by Nancy Schimmel.
       p.   cm.
    Translation of: Rädda min djungel.
    Summary: Eight-year-old Omar Castillo fulfills his dream of visiting the endangered rain
forest of southern Mexico and wins an audience with the president of Mexico to express
his concern.
    ISBN 0-912078-94-4 : $14.95
    1. Rain forest conservation—Mexico—Juvenile literature.
2. Deforestation—Control—Mexico—Juvenile literature.   3. Rain
forests—Mexico—Juvenile literature. [1. Rain forest
conservation—Mexico. 2. Rain forests—Mexico.] I. Runnerström,
Bengt-Arne, ill. II. Title.

SD418.3.M6Z3513   1992   91-40179
333.75'16'0971—dc20   CIP
                                                               AC

Volcano Press participates in the Cataloging in Publication Program of the Library of Congress. However, in our opinion, the data provided us for this book by CIP does not adequately nor accurately reflect its scope and content. Therefore, we are offering our librarian/users the choice between LC's treatment and an Alternative CIP prepared by Sanford Berman, Head Cataloger at Hennepin County Library, Edina, Minnesota.

Alternative Cataloging In Publication Data

Zak, Monica, 1939-

    Save my rainforest. Illustrated by Bengt-Arne
Runnerström; English version by Nancy Schimmel.
Volcano, CA: Volcano Press, copyright 1992.
    Translation of: Rädda min djungel.
    SUMMARY: Eight-year-old Omar Castillo visits the endangered Lacandona rainforest of
southern Mexico with his father and then starts a campaign to save it, including a talk
with the Mexican President and a demonstration in Mexico City's main square.

    1. Presidents—Mexico. 2. Eight-year-old boys—Mexico. 3. Lacandona Forest,
Mexico. 4. Child environmentalists—Mexico. 5. Rain forest conservation—Mexico.
6. Father and son—Mexico. 7. Rain forest movement—Mexico. 8. Rain forest
conservation—Protests, demonstrations, vigils, etc. 9. Children—Empowerment.
I. Title. II. Schimmel, Nancy, translator. III. Volcano Press. IV. Runnerström
Bengt-Arne, illus. V. Title: My rainforest.
335.7516

Books may be ordered directly from Volcano Press, P.O. Box 270, Volcano, CA 95689. Telephone: (209) 296-3445; FAX (209) 296-4515. Please enclose $14.95 for each copy. For postage and handling add $3.50 for the first book, and $1.00 for each additional book. California residents please add appropriate tax. For Teachers Resource Guide send $4.95 and a stamped self-addressed envelope.

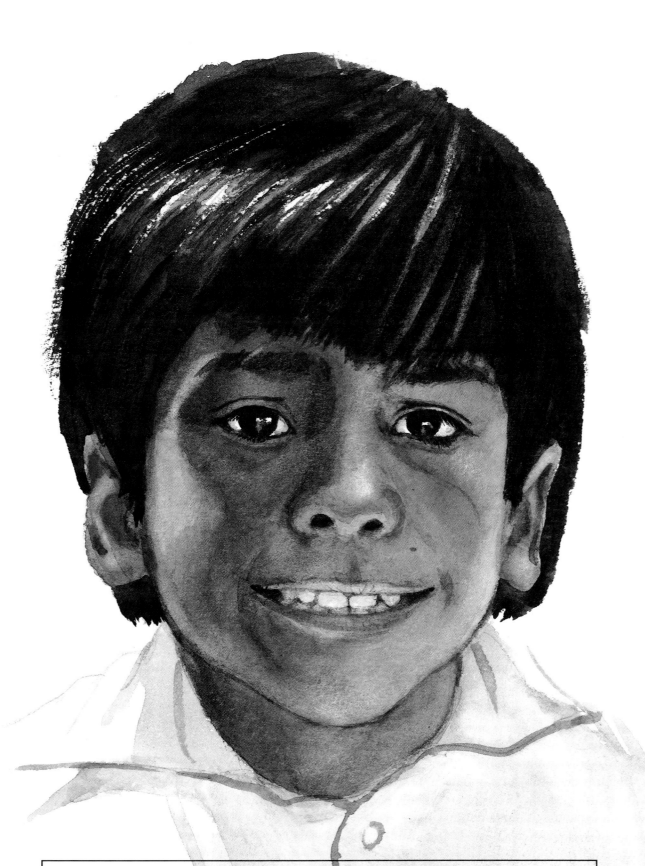

GLOSSARY

abuela—grandmother
arriba—hurray
fiesta de cumpleaños—birthday party
mango—tropical fruit

pozole—hominy soup
tortillas—corn or wheat flat bread
toucan—tropical bird
Zocalo—main square or plaza

Omar Castillo lives in Mexico City, the second biggest city in the world. It takes him over an hour by bus and subway to go visit his grandmother and grandfather. He can go by himself even though he is only eight years old.

But on the day this story begins, it is a wonder he gets home at all. His grandfather has been telling him about the rainforest in southern Mexico, and his head is so full he hardly notices where he is going. He imagines he is in the rainforest, among the huge trees, watching all the animals and tropical birds. The air is clear and clean. *When I grow up*, he thinks, *I will go there.*

Night has fallen by the time he gets off the bus and walks to the little house his family rents. His parents are already in bed.

His mother calls from the bedroom, "Are you hungry? There are bananas in the kitchen." He takes a banana. Then, for something to do while he eats, he turns on the TV.

The voice on the television says, "This is the last rainforest in Mexico, the Selva Lacandona." Omar nods; his grandfather told him that. "People have destroyed the others," continues the voice, "and now this one is threatened. The last rainforest in the country is about to disappear."

This can't be true, thinks Omar. But he sees it all clearly on the screen. The trees falling, burning, a deer desperately fleeing the fire. *My rainforest,* he thinks, *and I will never go there.*

"Mama!" Omar calls. "They are destroying my rainforest!"

"Papa," complains Omar, "the President won't answer my letters!"

Omar's father is tired. He has been working all day making hand-painted cards to sell at the market. "I don't want to hear any more about your rainforest!" he says.

"But we have to do something!"

"Well, go there yourself, then." Omar's father sounds annoyed, but Omar is happy. Of course! He should go to the rainforest.

The next morning at breakfast Omar asks, "Papa, why are they killing the rainforest?"

"I don't know," his father replies from behind his newspaper.

"But they shouldn't do it, Papa! I have to save the rainforest. But how?"

— "You could write a letter to the President," says his father, without looking up.

Of course. A letter to the President. Omar knows right where the President lives, downtown in the palace on the *Zocalo*. He goes there and gives his letter to the guard.

Every day he waits for the letter carrier, but nothing ever comes for him. He writes another letter. And another. And another. Still no answer.

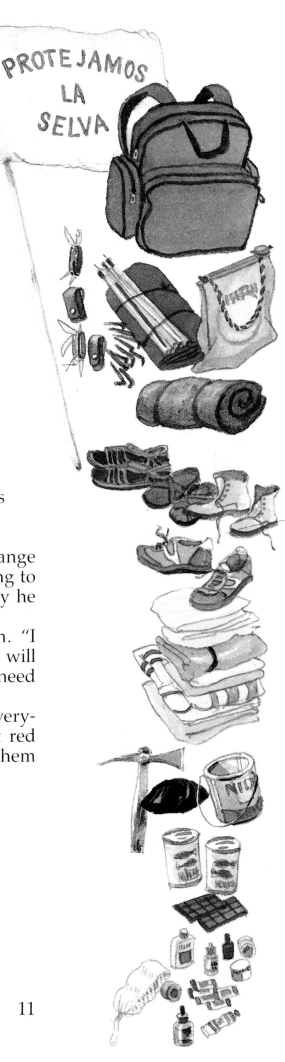

The next morning at three o'clock he goes to his parents' room to say goodbye. He has packed his knapsack with clean shirts and *tortillas* and a toothbrush, and he is ready to go.

"Wake up!" he says. "I'm going!"

"What? What? What's going on?" says his father sleepily.

"I'm going to the Lacandon Rainforest."

Finally his father really wakes up. He realizes Omar means what he says.

"Son, you can't do that. You don't know the way."

"I'll ask," says Omar calmly.

"It could be very dangerous," warns his father. "You will have to cross enormous rivers full of crocodiles."

"Doesn't matter. I'm going."

Omar's father talks and talks, trying to change Omar's mind, but Omar won't budge. He is going to the rainforest, and he tells his father exactly why he must go.

"All right," says Omar's father, with a sigh. "I will go with you. But wait. Your mother and I will have to do extra work so we can buy what we need for the trip."

At last his parents earn the money to buy everything Omar and his father need, from a bright red tent to bandages for blisters. His mother sews them a banner that says, "PROTEJAMOS LA SELVA."

11

Early one morning Omar and his father start walking. At first Omar is smiling and singing. On the road at last! And tonight, for the first time in his life, he will sleep in a tent.

For hours and hours they walk on the hot pavement. Finally, they leave the dirty yellow air of the city for the clear, clean air of the countryside. But Omar is too tired to notice. Then his feet begin to hurt. He goes a good ways before he says anything. When he does, his father stops and takes Omar's shoes off.

"You have blisters. I'll put a bandage on . . . there. Now we can get started again."

"But Papa, I'm too tired. I can't go on."

"I'm tired too," says his father, "but try to go a little farther. I'll buy us a cool drink at the next store." They find a fruit stand where a woman with long braids sells them tall glasses of pineapple drink.

She looks at them curiously and finally asks, "What does your banner say? I can't read."

Omar revives at once. "This side says 'Let's protect the rainforest' and the other side says 'Walk—Mexico City—Tuxtla Gutiérrez.' Tuxtla's a long way south of here, but that's where we decided to go, to see the governor of the state of Chiapas, where the rainforest is. He is responsible for taking care of it. We need to tell him to save the rainforest so there will still be a rainforest in Mexico for us children when we grow up."

"You must be sent from heaven!" she says.

Omar's father smiles. "No, he's just a regular kid. All kids have good ideas, but usually people don't listen to them. It never made any difference to me that they were destroying the rainforest and the animals, but when I thought about what my son said, I realized that he knew what he was talking about. That's why I decided to come with him."

13

Another day, the sun beats down through the thin mountain air. This time it is Omar's father who has blisters. He calls, "Must you walk so fast, Omar?"

After walking more than a week, they come down out of the mountains. They can see banana plantations now, and *mango* trees. They camp by the side of the road.

Omar lies in the tent and listens. The night before, he heard coyotes howling near the tent: ah-ooo, ah-ooo, ah-ooo. He was afraid. Now he listens to the murmuring leaves. *What if a snake should get into the tent? What if robbers attack us?* he thinks. An enormous truck rumbles past and shakes the tent. *What if the driver fell asleep and . . .*

"Omar, are you awake?" his father asks.

"Mm-hm," answers Omar. "I can't sleep."

"Well," says Omar's father, "we really had a tough day. Heat, no shade, and traffic. Now it's pleasant. We won't be cold tonight."

"No," says Omar, smiling. "Remember the first night in the tent? I thought it would be wonderful, camping, but then the rain started . . ."

"Yes," says his father, "and the water came in. At three in the morning! Remember how good that hot *pozole* tasted after we walked in the dark and cold?"

"Papa, how many more days do we have to walk?"

"I thought it would take fifteen or twenty days, but it will take much longer. I don't want to disappoint you, but I don't believe we can go on."

"But why?" asks Omar, astounded.

"We are running out of money."

They decide to keep going.

"We will have to beg for food," says Omar.

They go into a restaurant and Omar's father explains to the owner why they are walking. "We have no more money," Omar's father says, "and my son is awfully hungry." The owner turns them out without giving them even a glass of water. But then a woman sitting outside a little hut motions them in, makes a fresh pot of coffee, and serves them coffee and bread. It goes like that. Some days people give them food, but often they have to walk the whole day without eating anything. Those days are hard.

When Omar sees boys playing soccer, he stops and watches with envy, but they never ask him to play. Sometimes there are things to look at in the road: a huge scorpion or snakes run over by cars. But more often, walking is boring. Omar throws rocks at fenceposts, thinking *Why didn't I bring anything to play with?* Then somebody who hears he is going to the rainforest gives him a toy Tarzan. He passes the time pretending Tarzan is in the rainforest, swinging from vines.

People warn them not to take the shortest way to Tuxtla, the road that goes through poor villages. "They'll attack you and rob you. It's too dangerous!" But Omar and his father take that road anyway, because it is 125 miles shorter. At first they are a little afraid, but no one attacks them. In fact, women and children come out and give them oranges and *tortilla* chips.

18

On the morning of their twenty-fifth day of traveling, Omar's father wakes him with "Las Mananitas" on his harmonica. Omar had forgotten—today he is nine! His father gives him a big hug and kiss, but Omar can see that he is sad—there is no money for birthday presents. Then, in the afternoon, they come to a little village where the people have already heard about their walk to save the rainforest. When they find out it is Omar's birthday, a woman bakes him a cake and invites all the neighbors for a real *fiesta de cumpleaños.* The house is full of people. And the cake! It is enormous, and chocolate, and has nine candles.

Everyone says, "Omar, blow out the candles!" What a lucky day! Omar grins whipped cream and chocolate from ear to ear.

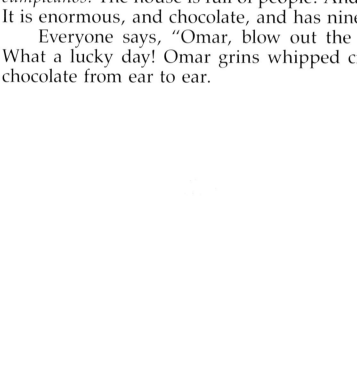

A few days later they stop in a little town to eat in a restaurant. An announcer comes on television to say there has been a terrible earthquake in Mexico City. They see a picture of a big pile of rubble and hear that it is the hospital where Omar's grandmother works! Omar starts to cry. His father has tears in his eyes. No one can reach Mexico City by telephone because the lines are out. Then a ham radio operator in the town promises he will help them get news.

After four days of waiting, the radio operator says, "Your *abuela* is alive, Omar. She wasn't in the hospital when the earthquake came. Your mother is well. She sends you kisses and says your house wasn't hurt at all. She wishes you a safe journey."

And now they can continue.

After thirty-nine days of walking, Omar and his father come to Tuxtla Gutiérrez. They have travelled 870 miles and they are tired. They have to wait the whole day outside the governor's office, but finally the moment comes that Omar has been hoping for.

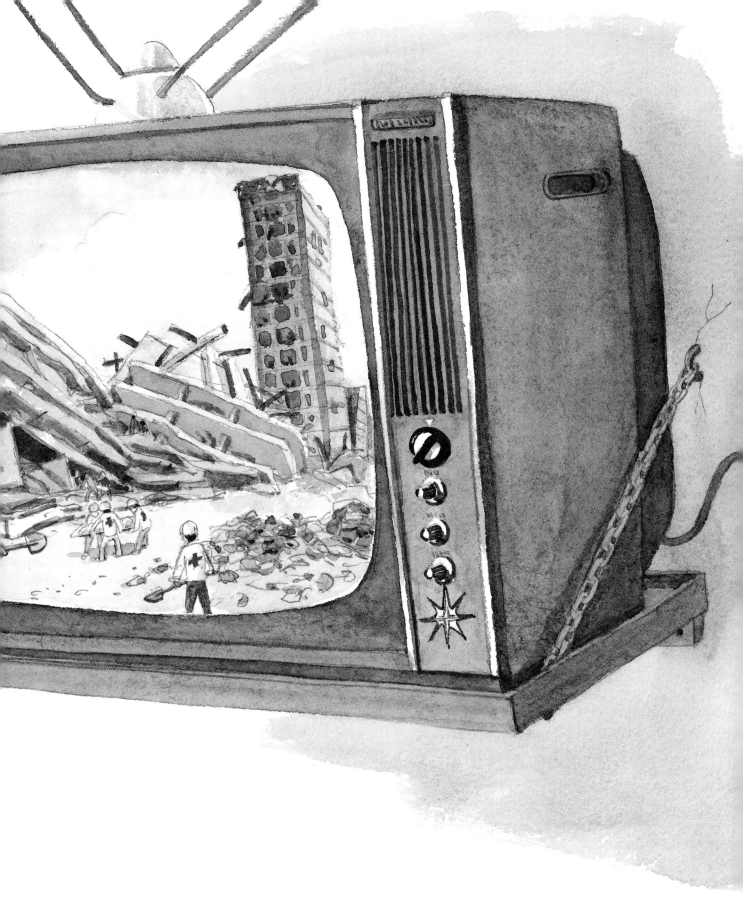

His heart beats loudly as he faces the governor and says, "Save my rainforest and stop the hunting of the rainforest animals for the next twenty years." The governor pats Omar on the head and says there is nothing to worry about.

Omar still worries. *He is treating me like a kid*, he thinks. *He won't do anything.*

But Omar
does get to see a
rainforest. When
Tuxtla was built, a
piece of the rainforest
was left as a park. At
first, Omar is disappointed
in the rainforest, too. There
aren't lots of strange animals
running around in plain sight. Just gigantic trees and a clean wet
smell.

Omar stands quietly for a long time in the deep green light
amid the huge trunks, listening to all the birds singing high above
in the canopy of leaves. Then he knows that being in a real rainforest at last is worth the trouble of walking 870 miles.

Omar and his father meet the zoologist, Don Miguel, who takes care of the park. Don Miguel explains, "They cut some of the trees for lumber, but mostly they are cutting the forest, and even burning some of the trees, to clear land to graze cattle. Every time somebody eats a hamburger, the people who cut down the rainforest get more money.

"You saw how dry the land is around Tuxtla. It's dry because the rainforest is gone. Cutting down the forest changes the climate. Now this little piece of rainforest has to be irrigated to preserve it. It's a rainforest without rain!"

Omar also learns that medicines come from the rainforest plants. More medicines could be found if the rainforests were left standing.

"I am old and tired," says Don Miguel to Omar's father. "I have been fighting all my life to save the rainforest. I don't have the strength to go on. So I am happy to know there are people like this boy. It gives me hope."

When Omar hears Don Miguel say this, he knows he can't give up. *I have to talk to the President,* he thinks. *After all, he is the one responsible for the whole country.*

When they get home, Omar goes to see the President. But it doesn't matter that he walked all the way to Tuxtla Gutiérrez to save the rainforest. The President will not see him.

So Omar and his father set up the little red tent under the President's balcony. Immediately a crowd gathers.

"Are you crazy?" they ask. "Why are you camping in the *Zocalo*?"

"Because I want to talk to the President," explains Omar, "and I won't leave until he listens to what I have to say."

All the cold December day, he marches around the huge plaza with his banner. By night, Omar's teeth are chattering, and still the President has not come out.

26

The next day, the newspapers run a story about Omar. More people come to see him.

Drivers give him the thumbs-up sign or call out to him, "*Arriba, Omar! We're with you! Save the rainforest!*"

That night, people Omar and his father don't even know come to guard them as they sleep.

Children come to play with Omar. They listen to the story of his walk. They make paper signs and start parading around the *Zocalo* with him.

"We will save the rainforest!" they shout at the top of their lungs. For four days.

Finally, Omar is so tired that he stops under the President's balcony and yells, "Señor Presidente! I am hungry and cold. Please let me come in. Señor Presidente, if you have children, think about them." No one appears on the balcony. Omar starts walking again. Two hundred times around the *Zocalo*. Then a man comes to tell Omar that the President wants to talk to him.

"Papa! It's happened!" shouts Omar, running to give his father a big hug. The children cheer as Omar goes into the palace. He knows he doesn't have much time so he just says the most important thing. He asks the President to save the last great rainforest of the country so it can be left to the children of Mexico as their inheritance.

The President promises Omar that in one year, the rainforest cutting will stop and nobody will be allowed to capture the rainforest birds and animals to sell them for pets.

Omar comes out of the presidential palace walking on air.

For a while, Omar is content, thinking that the President will save the rainforest.

A year later Omar goes to the Sonora Market in the center of the city. He looks at the beautiful toys, but he is really there to see the animals. In the corner of the huge marketplace where they sell pets, he finds a *toucan* in a cage.

The President had promised that no more rainforest creatures would be caught and sold, but he has broken his promise. Omar knows they are still cutting down the trees, too. "I promise to keep working to save your home," Omar says to the *toucan*, "and I will keep *my* promise."

Did you enjoy this story of the boy who wanted to save the rainforest? Well, it isn't a story. I am Omar Castillo. Now I am eleven; all that you read in this book happened when I was eight and nine.

I was very young then. I thought I had to do everything myself. I thought it would be enough to go and talk to the grown-ups who have the power to make decisions. I thought it would be enough just to say "Save my rainforest." Now I know this is not the way it works.

When I saw that they would keep destroying the rainforest, I went by bicycle to various states of Mexico. I asked the governors to write to the President asking him to protect the forests, but few of them agreed.

This showed me that I will not be able to save the rainforest by myself. It will take many of us to do that.

Now I have talked to many children in Mexico and I know that they think as I do: all children want a rainforest to be there when we grow up. And all the children I have talked to are as determined as I am. If the grown-ups don't stop cutting the Lacandon Rainforest, we will all have to go there; hundreds of thousands of children will make a chain that will surround the rainforest. And we will not move until they stop logging!

To the reader: If you want to find out more about how to help rainforests, and other environmental projects, send a stamped, self-addressed envelope to: Rainforest, Volcano Press, PO Box 270, Volcano, CA 95689.

DISCARDED
FROM
LIU LIBRARY